# SALEM, MASSACHUSETTS

*Examination of a Witch* by T. H. Matteson, 1853

# SALEM, MASSACHUSETTS

DILLON PRESS
Parsippany, New Jersey

by Deborah Kent

## Photo Credits

Front cover: Owen Franken/Stock Boston; back cover: Jim McElholm. Maps by Ortelius Design. David Binder/Stock Boston: 54; Jim McAllister: 51, 55; Courtesy, National Park Service: 46, 47, 49; Peabody Essex Museum, Salem, MA: 2-3, 11, 15, 23 (detail), 35, 43 (detail), 48, 50 (detail), 56; Michael Powell: 39; Courtesy, Salem Witch Museum: 9, 29.

## Library of Congress Cataloging-in-Publication Data

Kent, Deborah.
    Salem, Massachusetts/by Deborah Kent.—1st ed.
    p.    cm.—(Places in American history)
  Includes index.
  ISBN 0–87518–648–3 (LSB).—ISBN 0–382–39174–8 (pbk.)
    1. Witchcraft—Massachusetts—Salem—History—Juvenile literature. 2. Trials (Witchcraft)—Massachusetts—Salem—Juvenile literature. 3. Salem (Mass.)—History—Juvenile literature. 4. Salem (Mass.)—Social conditions—Juvenile literature. [1. An account of the events leading up to and during the legendary witchcraft trials in Salem Massachusetts, and a look at Salem's place in history after 1693 and at the historical sites that tourists can visit today. 2. Witchcraft—Massachusetts—Salem. 3. Trials (Witchcraft)—Massachusetts—Salem. 4. Salem (Mass.)] I. Title. II. Series.
  BF1575.K46 1996
133.4'3'097445—dc20                       95–13276

Summary: A detailed account of the events that led to and occurred during the legendary witchcraft trials in Salem, Massachusetts. Includes a look at Salem's place in history after 1693 and the historical sites that tourists can visit today.

 Published by Dillon Press,
A Division of Simon & Schuster,
299 Jefferson Road, Parsippany, NJ 07054

First Edition

Printed in the United States of America

10 9 8 7 6 5 4 3 2 1

# CONTENTS

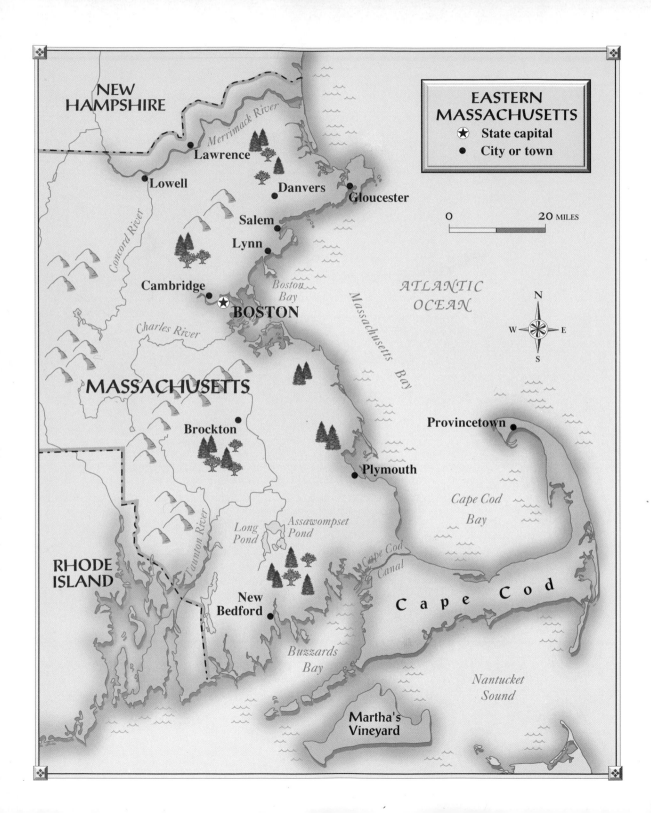

NEW HAMPSHIRE

Merrimack River

Lawrence

Lowell

Danvers

Gloucester

Salem

Lynn

Concord River

Cambridge

★ BOSTON

Boston Bay

Charles River

Massachusetts Bay

ATLANTIC OCEAN

MASSACHUSETTS

Brockton

Provincetown

Plymouth

Cape Cod Bay

Long Pond

Assawompset Pond

Taunton River

Cape Cod Canal

RHODE ISLAND

New Bedford

Cape Cod

Buzzards Bay

Nantucket Sound

Martha's Vineyard

EASTERN MASSACHUSETTS
★ State capital
● City or town

0    20 MILES

N
W    E
S

# CHAPTER 1

# TALES BY THE FIRE

Every morning, Abigail Williams waited on her invalid aunt, carrying trays of food and pots of tea up the narrow stairs to the sickroom. Abigail spent her afternoons at the spinning wheel in the parlor. Meanwhile, her cousin, Betty Parris, did almost no chores around the house. Betty was so frail and sickly that no one demanded much work from her. But Abigail was sturdy and blooming with good health. Besides, she was an orphan who had been taken in by her uncle, the Reverend Samuel Parris of Salem Village, Massachusetts. Abigail was expected to earn her keep at the parsonage.

Winter days passed slowly in Salem Village (the present-day town of Danvers). Salem Town, a thriving fishing port on the coast, was eight long miles away. A journey to the city of Boston, with its shops and crowds of people, meant another twenty miles over muddy roads and tangled forest paths. Reverend Parris would never approve of a trip to the city just for fun. He didn't even like the girls to play tag or hide-and-seek. He said that playing was a sign of idleness, and idleness gave the Devil a chance to do his work.

The only time twelve-year-old Abigail and nine-year-old Betty really enjoyed themselves was in the evening. While Reverend Parris worked on sermons in his study, the girls sat in the snug kitchen by the fire and talked with Tituba. Tituba, a woman of mixed African and Native American ancestry, was Reverend Parris's slave. Not many people in Salem Village owned slaves, but the Reverend had bought Tituba and her husband, John Indian, while on a trip to the island of Barbados in the West Indies.

On cold winter evenings, Tituba told the girls about tropical birds and flowers and smooth,

*Tituba loved to tell fantastic stories to the girls at the parsonage.*

sandy beaches warmed by the sun. Sometimes, too, she told them tales she had heard years ago from some of the older slaves on the island. These stories were of animals that could talk and evil demons that preyed on children at night. Tituba's stories came from faraway Africa, the homeland of some of her ancestors.

The strange, magical tales filled the girls with excitement. When the wind howled eerily outside the kitchen door, the girls felt little prickles of fear run up their spines, and they shivered.

In bed at night, they lay awake for a long time. The girls whispered in the dark about monkeys and spiders that spoke like human beings and weird hunching figures that might lurk in the shadows.

In 1692, when Betty and Abigail were growing up, people of the Massachusetts Bay Colony were strict Puritans. Puritanism was a stern, unsmiling religion. Its followers believed in a God who punished wrongdoers and a Devil who was always waiting to lead the unwary astray. The teachings of the Bible guided everyday life.

Just as Tituba brought African stories to Massachusetts, the Puritan colonists brought with them a set of ancient beliefs from Europe. These beliefs helped people explain events that they could not understand in any other way. According to stories told by parents to their children through the centuries, the Devil could persuade ordinary women and men to be his servants. Drawing on Satan's power, these servants could turn milk sour, make hens stop

*A kitchen hearth and utensils as they would have looked in the seventeenth century*

laying eggs, and bring sickness to a healthy child. The men who did the Devil's bidding were known as wizards, and the women were called witches.

As the winter dragged on, other girls joined Betty and Abigail in the parsonage kitchen. Some were the daughters of farmers and tradesmen. Others were servants, stealing an hour or two of hard-won leisure. Like Betty and Abigail, they all enjoyed Tituba's magical tales. Sometimes, just for fun, they told each other's fortunes by dropping an egg white into a glass of water and interpreting the picture it seemed to form.

Looking back, you might say that trouble sprang from these games of fortunetelling or from Tituba's haunting tales. Or perhaps trouble began because of the stifled spirits of girls who longed for fun and adventure but found only boredom, hard work, and warnings about Satan. Whatever its cause, trouble arrived in January 1692 when Betty Parris began to have strange "spells" or fits. She stared into space and did not answer when her parents called her. Within a few weeks, Abigail, too, was behaving in ways no one could explain. Like her cousin, she stared blankly and did not answer when spoken to. Sometimes she fell to the floor, writhing and screaming as though she were in pain.

Soon the other girls who came to the parsonage were stricken with the same mysterious fits of kicking and shrieking. They said they were being burned or pricked with needles or pinched by unseen fingers. One eyewitness described their attacks: "Their arms, necks, and backs were turned this way and that, and returned back again, so as it was impossible for them to do of themselves, and beyond the power of any epileptic's fit or natural disease."

At last, Reverend Parris called in a doctor to examine Betty and Abigail. Dr. William Griggs could find nothing physically wrong with the girls. There was only one explanation for their strange behavior. It was obvious, the doctor declared, that Betty and Abigail were under the spell of a witch.

# CHAPTER 2

# "THOU SHALT NOT SUFFER A WITCH TO LIVE"

"Witchcraft: what shall I say of it?" wrote the Boston minister Cotton Mather in 1689. "It is the furthest effort of our original sin, and all that can make any practice or person odious is here in the exaltation of it."

Cotton Mather was one of the most respected clergymen in Puritan Massachusetts. He was highly educated and wrote about all the social and religious issues of his time. One of the topics that intrigued him was witchcraft.

Like most people in colonial New England, Cotton Mather believed that certain people used magic to help the Devil in his evil work. Yet he warned that the evidence against anyone

*In this picture an accused witch reacts with horror as her accuser points a finger.*

suspected of using magic must be weighed very carefully. There was always the danger that an innocent person might be accused of witchcraft, one of the highest crimes in the colonies.

In 1688, Mather observed a case of witchcraft that appeared to be thoroughly genuine. A Boston mason named John Goodwin asked Mather to examine his four children, who seemed to be possessed by some evil force. Several times a day they fell to the floor, screaming and rolling about. The children also refused to eat. When Reverend Mather prayed over them, they covered their ears as though they could not bear to hear the sacred words.

Shortly before these attacks began, thirteen-year-old Martha Goodwin and her eleven-year-old brother, John, had gone to collect the family laundry from an Irish washerwoman, the widow Glover. After receiving the clean clothes, the children protested that some were missing. Widow Glover was outraged. She cursed the children and told them they would suffer for accusing her of stealing. Soon afterward, the children's strange fits began and later spread to their two younger siblings.

After observing the children and questioning Widow Glover, Cotton Mather was convinced that this was a case of witchcraft. He believed that the washerwoman had put a curse on the Goodwin children, causing their convulsions and their dread of Holy Scripture. A Boston court agreed, and Widow Glover went to the gallows.

Today it is hard to understand how a woman could be hanged for losing her temper with a couple of children. But we must remember the harsh realities of life in the seventeenth century. Calamity constantly hovered over the people of Massachusetts. Without warning, smallpox could wipe out an entire family; a band of Indians could sweep out of the forest to raid a nearby town; or bad weather might ruin the season's harvest. To a struggling Puritan farmer, even the death of a cow was a catastrophe.

The Puritans believed that any such disaster might be punishment from God. But for many there existed the possibility that a witch or a wizard was to blame. Many seventeenth-century New Englanders believed that the evil deeds of witches or wizards, labeled witchcraft, posed a serious danger to their lives and property. In the 60 years before 1692, sixteen people were hanged as witches in Massachusetts and Connecticut.

In the 1600s, witchcraft was believed to fall into three categories. A white witch used spells and potions for harmless purposes—to predict the future or to heal the sick. Black witches, on the other hand, used magic to cause hardship or injury. Their spells could make a roof leak, wither crops in a field, or even cause a child to fall ill and die. In the most extreme form of witchcraft, the witch made a contract, or pact, with the Devil. In exchange for power or wealth, the witch became the Devil's servant and willingly worked his mischief on earth.

Some historians claim that witchcraft, or the black arts as it became known, was never actually practiced in Massachusetts. Others point out that witchcraft, in one form or another, has been used around the world and by many different cultures throughout the ages. It does not seem far-fetched to suspect that in colonial New England, where nearly everyone believed in witchcraft, at least a few people may have tried to use it. Some may have experimented with magic in hopes of curing the sick or punishing a meddling neighbor, for example.

Scientists have shown that people who practice magic can wield very real power. Most experts think that this power is based on the strong beliefs of the person who is bewitched. For example, a sick child may get better if she thinks that the healer's spells are doing her good, or a man who believes that a fatal curse has been put upon him may actually get sick and die.

The Goodwin children, after hearing the widow Glover's threats, were probably convinced that something terrible was about to happen to them. Their "fits" grew out of their fears—fears based on the beliefs of the society in which they lived.

Cotton Mather warned that no one should be convicted of witchcraft without that person being carefully investigated first. But when a supposed witch was discovered, Mather and most other Puritan ministers turned to the Bible for guidance. They repeated the words of Exodus 22:18—"Thou shalt not suffer a witch to live."

# CHAPTER 3

# POINTING FINGERS

Reverend Parris was shocked when Dr. Griggs voiced his belief that Betty and Abigail were suffering the effects of witchcraft. How had such a thing happened in his own house—to his own daughter and niece? With ministers from nearby towns, Reverend Parris prayed over the girls and repeatedly asked them who was causing their terrible convulsions. But Betty and Abigail could not name the person who was tormenting them.

As the days passed, the families of the afflicted girls grew frantic. Then late in February, Mary Sibley, the aunt of one of the sufferers, decided to draw out the truth with a bit of harmless white magic. She instructed Tituba and her husband, John Indian, to prepare a "witch cake." Following an ancient English recipe, the cake was made from flour mixed with the girls' urine. John and Tituba baked the cake at the parsonage, and, as was the custom, fed it to a dog. Mary Sibley believed that this ritual would somehow help the girls visualize who was hurting them.

When he learned that a witch cake had been baked in his own kitchen, Reverend Parris was horrified. But the witch cake seemed to work its magic. After lengthy questioning, the girls revealed their tormentors' names at last.

Betty Parris was the first to speak. Sobbing with terror, she told her father that Tituba had bewitched her. Soon some of the other girls spoke out as well. They named, or "cried out upon," two more Salem Village women—Sarah Good and Sarah Osborne.

Sarah Osborne was an elderly woman in failing health. She had not gone to church in 14 months—a sin in Puritan Massachusetts. Sarah Good was a homeless woman who slept in haylofts and begged from door to door. When people turned her away, she wandered off and muttered under her breath. People said that cows sometimes died after Sarah was turned away.

All three accused witches were women who were different from others in the community. One was a slave from the West Indies and the other two were free women of doubtful character. If there were witches in Salem Village, these three seemed to be likely suspects.

On March 1, two magistrates, John Hathorne and Jonathan Corwin, rode the eight miles from Salem Town to Salem Village to question the suspected witches. Farmers, blacksmiths, servants, and children crowded into the Salem Village Meetinghouse to see the excitement. In the front row sat Abigail Williams, Betty Parris, and six other girls who had experienced the strange convulsions. They were the star witnesses in the case. From time to time, as the accused women spoke, the girls tumbled to the floor, writhing and screaming.

*In this drawing from* Harper's New Monthly Magazine, *December 1892, an accuser claims to see a flock of yellow birds around the head of an accused witch.*

Judge Hathorne did most of the questioning, while Judge Corwin quietly took notes. Hathorne demanded to know why the accused women had hurt these poor children. Didn't they see the terrible pain they were causing? But even under such harsh questioning, Sarah Good and Sarah Osborne insisted that they had done nothing wrong.

Tituba, on the other hand, launched into a confession that lasted for three full days. Perhaps she really thought of herself as a witch—or perhaps she hoped the judges would be lenient if she told them what they wanted to hear. Whatever her reasons, Tituba stated that she was the Devil's servant. She described red rats and talking cats and claimed that a tall man dressed in black had demanded that she make her mark in a great book. Tituba said that Sarah Good, Sarah Osborne, and others, whose names she could not read, had signed the book as well. The people of Salem Village listened, fascinated and appalled.

When Tituba's spectacular confession was finally over, all three prisoners were taken to Boston Jail to await formal trial. There, in a cold, damp cell, Sarah Osborne died of natural causes two months later.

The capture of the three suspected witches did nothing to cure Abigail Williams and the other girls. Day by day their fits grew more violent. People wondered about the unknown names Tituba had seen in the tall man's book. Somewhere, they believed, more witches still walked free.

In the middle of March, one of the afflicted girls, twelve-year-old Anne Putnam, made a shocking announcement. The name of another witch had come to her. This time the accused was not an outcast, but a solid citizen named Martha Corey.

Martha Corey went to church every Sunday, but she was not popular in Salem Village. She was outspoken and opinionated. When Martha Corey learned that she had been accused of witchcraft, she laughed out loud. Her laughter was enough to convince some people that she must be guilty.

The next person accused of witchcraft, 71-year-old Rebecca Nurse, seemed completely above suspicion. Rebecca was kind and generous—beloved by her family and neighbors. Yet Anne Putnam and some of the other girls claimed that Rebecca had floated into their rooms at night, pinching and torturing them. It was widely believed that a witch's spirit, or spectral shape, could leave her body and wander about the countryside, causing trouble.

When four church members told Rebecca Nurse that she had been accused of witchcraft, she insisted that she was innocent. "What sin has God found in me unrepented of," she asked humbly, "that he should lay such an affliction upon me in my old age?" But like Tituba and the others, Rebecca Nurse was taken to jail to await trial.

In the months that followed, more girls and young women all over northeastern Massachusetts began to have writhing fits. Today many scientists and historians think that these girls may have had a form of mental illness called hysteria. The mental state of a person with hysteria can cause very real physical symptoms even though the person's body is perfectly healthy. For example, someone with hysteria may become blind, deaf, or paralyzed, even though there is nothing wrong with his or her eyes, ears, or legs. A person with hysteria may think that he or she is being burned or bitten and then develop actual blisters or tooth marks.

Convinced that witches were torturing them, the girls of Salem Village jerked and twisted in hysterical convulsions. In a phenomenon known as group hysteria, the strange illness spread from one girl to another as swiftly as an idea leaps from one mind to the next.

Many of the girls seemed to have been in very real distress. But others may have enjoyed all the attention and excitement. As they screamed and flailed, the girls were at center stage, and people devoured every word they uttered. One of the girls admitted that her behavior had become a kind of game. When asked why she had cried out upon a neighbor, she replied, "It was for sport. I must have some sport."

Not everyone believed the afflicted girls told the truth. One of the doubters was a Salem farmer named John Procter. When one of his servants, Mary Warren, began to have fits, he sat her down at the spinning wheel and threatened to beat her unless she behaved herself. For a time Mary's fits disappeared. Procter argued that if the girls had their way, soon everyone around them would be accused of witchcraft. He suggested that the girls themselves were the real demons and that they ought to be punished. Soon John Procter and his wife Elizabeth were both accused of practicing witchcraft. They joined the growing crowd in Boston Jail.

As the witch hunt raged on, Massachusetts jails overflowed with suspects. The youngest prisoner was Dorcas Good, Sarah Good's five-year-old

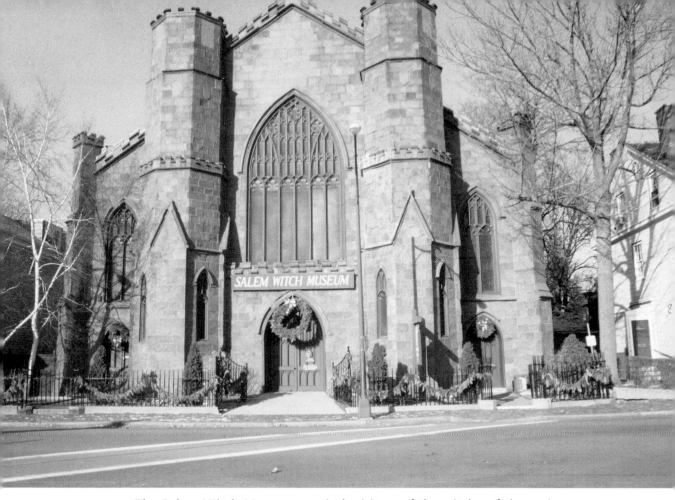

*The Salem Witch Museum reminds visitors of the witchcraft hysteria that took place in Salem Village in 1692 and 1693.*

daughter. When an official questioned her, Dorcas said that she had a little snake that talked to her and sucked blood from her finger. She showed him a red spot on her finger to prove it. Perhaps, like many children, Dorcas had an imaginary playmate—one in keeping with all the strange grown-up talk that buzzed around her.

But to the frenzied people of Salem Village, her little snake was a "familiar," a witch's spirit companion and servant.

Perhaps the most unlikely suspect of all was George Burroughs, who had once served as pastor of the church in Salem Village. Burroughs had left the village in 1683 and now lived in Maine. Yet Anne Putnam claimed that he had appeared to her in a dream and told her that he was master of all the witches in Massachusetts. The officials listened soberly to Anne's story. They rationalized that if Burroughs was in league with Satan, then it was possible for his spectral shape to visit Anne Putnam in a dream.

One day as he sat at dinner with his family, George Burroughs heard a knock at his door. A band of men from Salem Town stood outside and announced that he was under arrest. Burroughs scarcely had time to tell his wife and children goodbye. Within minutes he was on his way to jail—to await trial with so many others for the mysterious crime called witchcraft.

# CHAPTER 4

# THE BLACK ARTS ON TRIAL

**B**y the end of May 1692, nearly 200 accused witches and wizards were locked in Massachusetts jails. Some, like Tituba, confessed that they were indeed the servants of Satan. The people who confessed were forgiven and eventually released. But most of the people accused of practicing witchcraft insisted that they were innocent. Their fate rested in the hands of the court at Salem Town.

Like George Burroughs, many of the suspected witches were jailed solely on the basis of spectral evidence. In such cases a witness claimed to have seen the accused person's spirit or spectral shape in a dream. At the time, the person's physical body may have been miles away.

Reverend Cotton Mather of Boston warned that spectral evidence was very unreliable. He suggested that the Devil might make mischief by taking the shape of an innocent person. The afflicted girls might not be seeing the accused witches in their dreams but the disguised form of Satan himself. Despite these warnings the judges who presided at Salem Town decided to accept spectral evidence in the courtroom.

There was no need for spectral evidence in the first trial, held at the Salem Town Meetinghouse on June 2, 1692. The accused witch was a woman named Bridget Bishop. For years her neighbors had suspected her of practicing the black arts. Workmen testified that, while renovating her cellar, they had found several strange-looking dolls buried in a wall. The dolls were stuck all over with pins, and some were missing their heads. It was widely believed that witches used dolls to perform magic rituals—rituals that could injure their victims. The jury found Bridget Bishop guilty of practicing witchcraft. On June 10 she was hanged not far from the Meetinghouse, on a rise of land called Gallows Hill.

On June 30, five more people went on trial in Salem, including Sarah Good and Rebecca Nurse. In these cases there were no dolls full of pins, and the judges had to rely almost entirely on spectral evidence. Shrieking and writhing, the afflicted girls swore that the shapes of the accused witches pinched, burned, and tortured them. Without hesitation the jury convicted four of the five suspects. It was declared that gentle Rebecca Nurse was innocent.

The moment the jurors announced that Rebecca Nurse could go free, the girls broke into ear-splitting howls and screeches. They rolled on the floor, kicking and thrashing. The courtroom was in an uproar. At last the judges asked the jury to reconsider its decision. The jury left the room and returned with a new verdict—Rebecca Nurse was guilty after all.

Rebecca Nurse and the four other condemned prisoners were hanged on July 19, 1692. Just before Sarah Good went to the gallows, Reverend Nicholas Noyes of Salem Town urged her to confess. "I am no more a witch than you are a wizard," she replied, "and if you take away my life, God will give you blood to drink." According to legend, Reverend Noyes died of a hemorrhage 25 years later, choking on his own blood.

Through the long, terrible summer of 1692, Massachusetts was swept up in a deadly witch hunt. More and more people began having convulsions—and more and more people were arrested. Some of the most powerful and respected people in the colony, including merchants, clergymen, and judges, were arrested. No one could be trusted and no one was safe. The very fabric of society seemed to be unraveling.

Five more convicted prisoners were hanged on August 19. Among them was John Procter, the farmer who had warned Salem against listening to the tormented girls. Another was the former Salem Village pastor, George Burroughs. Just before his execution, Burroughs faced the gaping

*In this painting you can see the tormented girls pointing their fingers in accusation.*

spectators and recited the Lord's Prayer. Most people believed that a wizard or witch could not say the Lord's Prayer without making a mistake. But Burroughs delivered the familiar words flaw-lessly, in a clear, ringing voice. Then he turned away and mounted the gallows. Was it possible, people wondered uneasily, that an innocent man had been sent to his death?

The trial of Giles Corey was set for mid-September 1692. Giles was the husband of Martha Corey, who had been convicted and hanged earlier. He was a weather-beaten New England farmer, nearly 80 years old. In his slow, stolid way, Giles Corey conceived a plan to outwit the judges. When they questioned him about devilish practices, he simply refused to speak.

According to the law, Giles Corey could not be tried if he refused to testify. But the court had methods for making people talk. In a field near the Meetinghouse, Corey was tied hand and foot. Then, one by one, heavy stones were piled upon his chest. He was told that if he would answer the court's questions, the stones would be removed. But Giles Corey never gave in. The only words he gasped out were, "More weight! More weight!" After two days of this slow torture, he died.

On September 22, eight more convicted witches were hanged in Salem Town. One of them was Mary Easty, the younger sister of Rebecca Nurse. Shortly before her death, she sent a letter to the judges and clergymen involved with the witchcraft trials.

"I petition to Your Honors not for my own life," she wrote, ". . . but that no more innocent blood be shed. . . By my own innocence, I know you are in the wrong way. . . . I beg Your Honors not to deny this humble petition from a poor, dying, innocent person, and question not that the Lord will give blessing to your endeavors."

George Burroughs's prayer and Mary Easty's heartfelt letter forced many people to take a hard look at the trials. The witch hunt that began in Salem Village was now out of control. By October, most of the judges, ministers, and ordinary people of Massachusetts believed that innocent men and women had died. Reverend Increase Mather, Cotton Mather's father, told the Boston clergy, "It were better that ten suspected witches should escape than that one innocent person should be condemned."

On October 12, Massachusetts Governor Sir William Phips issued an order to protect the remaining prisoners "from any wrong which might be done to them." He also ordered that no more suspected witches should be arrested unless it was absolutely necessary.

The last witch trials were held in January 1693. Three more people were convicted but none of them was hanged. Little by little the passion of the witch hunt subsided. People began to ignore the shrieks and pointing fingers of the afflicted girls. Eventually their convulsions disappeared. Farmers went back to their neglected fields, and life slipped into order once more.

Nineteen women and men were hanged at Salem in 1692, and one man died by torture.

*This stone marker is a memorial to Susannah Martin, who was hanged July 19, 1692.*

Hundreds of other lives were shattered beyond repair. The government had confiscated the property of the convicted witches, leaving their families penniless. Even after the trials were over, dozens of prisoners languished for months in jail. Since prisoners were required to pay for their food and board, they could not be released until someone handed over the money for their expenses.

In the years after 1692, Massachusetts staggered under a series of epidemics and crop failures. Many people feared that God was punishing them for the hangings at Salem. On January 14, 1697, Salem held a day of fasting and prayer, asking for the Lord's forgiveness.

Few clues have survived to tell us what became of the girls whose accusations started the Salem witch hunt. Records reveal that Betty

Parris eventually married and had children. But no clues of Abigail Williams's life remain.

At least one of the afflicted girls later tried to atone for the harm she had done. On a Sunday in August 1706, Anne Putnam rose at her pew in Salem Village Meetinghouse. From the pulpit the pastor read a statement that Anne had carefully prepared. She asked for forgiveness from the families of the people she had accused, from the congregation, and from God himself. Solemnly, the pastor read Anne Putnam's words.

> "I desire to be humbled before God.
> It was a great delusion of Satan that
> deceived me in that sad time. I did it not
> out of any anger, malice, or ill will. . . .
> I desire to lie in the dust and earnestly
> beg forgiveness of all those I have given
> just cause of sorrow and offense, and
> whose relations were taken away and
> accused."

For more than three centuries, the Salem Village witchcraft trials have captured the American imagination. The witch hunt has been portrayed in poetry and fiction, drama and motion picture. Yet the tragic events of 1692 form only one episode in Salem's long and colorful past. Far more important to history is Salem Town's rise as an international port of trade—a town that sent ships to the farthest edges of the world.

CHAPTER 5

# SALEM COMES OF AGE

**W**henever a ship sailed into Salem Harbor, people flocked to the wharves. They were eager to welcome the returning sailors and to see what cargo the ship carried home from distant lands. On a summer day in 1795, the crowd seemed more excited than it ever had before. Down the gangplank of a ship just back from India lumbered an enormous beast. It had huge, flapping ears and a long nose that curled like a snake. The ground shook as it stepped ashore.

The elephant that arrived that day in 1795 was the first ever to set foot on American soil. Why did such a momentous event occur in the little town of Salem, Massachusetts? What made Salem so special?

Long before the first Europeans arrived, the sea was vital to the people who lived along the northern coast of present-day Massachusetts. The native Americans called the Salem region *Naumkeag*, meaning "the fishing place." The first European settlers reached today's Salem in 1626 and were followed by a larger group that sailed from England two years later. These early Puritan settlers found it difficult to farm the stony New England soil. Many turned to the sea

*Crowninshield's Wharf in Salem as it appeared around 1800*

for their livelihood, harvesting the rich schools of cod, halibut, and other fish that flourished along the coast.

As the years passed, Salem fishermen built larger boats and their expeditions carried them farther and farther from home. By 1692, when the condemned witches were being hanged on Gallows Hill, Salem fishing fleets were traveling as far north as Nova Scotia, in Canada. Merchants found eager markets for dried cod in Virginia and other southern colonies and also in the Caribbean Islands. The cod business brought wealth to many merchants in Salem and other Massachusetts towns and earned them the nickname "the codfish aristocracy."

During the 1700s, Boston became a major center for trade in the British colonies. Salem, Boston's smaller neighbor to the north, also grew and prospered. Salem shipbuilders designed vessels that could withstand the rigors of long ocean voyages. Merchant ships from Salem crossed the Atlantic to trade with the nations along the Baltic Sea—Germany, Denmark, and Russia. Salem's ships explored the Mediterranean to initiate trade with Spain and North Africa. Then in 1786 a merchant named Elias Hasket Derby sent a ship named *Grand Turk* on a daring mission around Africa's Cape of Good Hope, across the Indian Ocean, and all the way to China.

*Grand Turk*'s voyage was a spectacular success. Derby tripled the money he had invested in the project. Soon other Salem merchants followed his example. Loaded with New England merchandise such as lumber and dried codfish, ships set out from tiny Salem to circle the globe in quest of trade. After months or even years at sea, they hove into port again, heavy with Spanish wine, ivory from India, Sumatran coffee, and tea and silks from China.

Salem's waterfront rang with the shouts of dockworkers as they unloaded cargo. The wharves were piled with casks of wine, bales of silk, cotton cloth, and barrels of molasses. The mingled smells of tar, coffee, pepper, and spices

*Elias Hasket Derby, Salem's most successful merchant, could well afford this brick house and the costly furnishings inside.*

hung in the air. Customs officials dragged giant scales to the wharves and carefully weighed each carton and bundle before it could be hauled ashore. In the shipyards nearby rose the wooden skeletons of new vessels that would soon carry the name of Salem to the shores of Africa and Asia.

Not every ship came safely home again. Countless young men from Salem disappeared into Davy Jones' locker, as the sailors nicknamed the bottom of the sea. A fierce Atlantic storm

*The study of the Elias Hasket Derby house*

could snap the masts of a schooner and spill its men into the icy water. Pirates preyed on merchant vessels, stealing the cargo and murdering the crew. Even within sight of land, a ship might be wrecked upon hidden rocks. After a near collision with another ship, one sailor wrote in his diary, "David Jones did not get us this time, though we are consigned to his locker one of these days."

If a ship was lost, with all its valuable cargo and crew, its owner could lose a fortune. But the Salem merchants were not afraid to take risks, and many grew rich. During the late 1700s and early 1800s, merchant families such as the Derbys and Crowninshields built elegant houses on Essex and Chestnut streets in Salem. Their

homes overflowed with beautiful teakwood
tables, mahogany chests, painted Chinese fans,
elephants carved from ivory, and other treasures
from around the world.

For two decades after Elias Derby first
opened the China trade in 1786, Salem Town was
home port to some 250 sailing ships. It was one
of the nation's most important seaports, second
only to Boston. By 1800, Salem had the highest

*Goods of all kinds were brought to Salem in the late 1700s and
early 1800s by sailing vessels returning from ports around the world.*

*The United States Custom House, completed in 1819, was the place where officials could inspect documents and cargoes brought in from foreign lands.*

per capita income (averaged out for each person) of any American city.

In 1800 the United States was a young nation, newly independent from Great Britain. Its rising power was a threat to Great Britain and France, and international tension mounted. Many American merchant ships were attacked by French and English vessels. In 1807, President Thomas Jefferson closed all ports in the United States to foreign trade. Jefferson's Embargo Act changed the port of Salem forever.

For almost two years, Salem's proud ships floated at anchor, their sails furled. The Derbys, Crowninshields, and other merchants looked for

*By 1854, Salem was a bustling port as well as a place where factories were being built.*

other ways to make money. Many invested in textile factories in nearby towns. When the embargo was lifted and Salem vessels set sail again, the merchants divided their attention between overseas trade and the growing textile industry at home. As the years passed, steam-powered ships gradually replaced sailing vessels. Although the steamships looked clumsy, the merchants liked them because they were fast and reliable. The grace and beauty of sailing ships yielded to the efficiency of the new technology.

In 1870 the three-masted bark *Glide* sailed into Salem Harbor after a long journey. It was

*The central wharves at Salem today*

the last of the sail-powered ships to return to Salem after a voyage from Zanzibar, beyond the Cape of Good Hope. Its return marked the end of Salem's 200-year history as a sailing town.

During the early twentieth century, Salem continued to grow as a busy factory town. Today the town still carries many reminders of its long and fascinating history. Museums preserve original documents that have survived since the witchcraft trials of 1692. Elegant houses on Essex and Chestnut streets are the legacy of the powerful merchant families of the 1700s. For visitors, Salem is a place where the past and the present blend together and history seems to come alive.

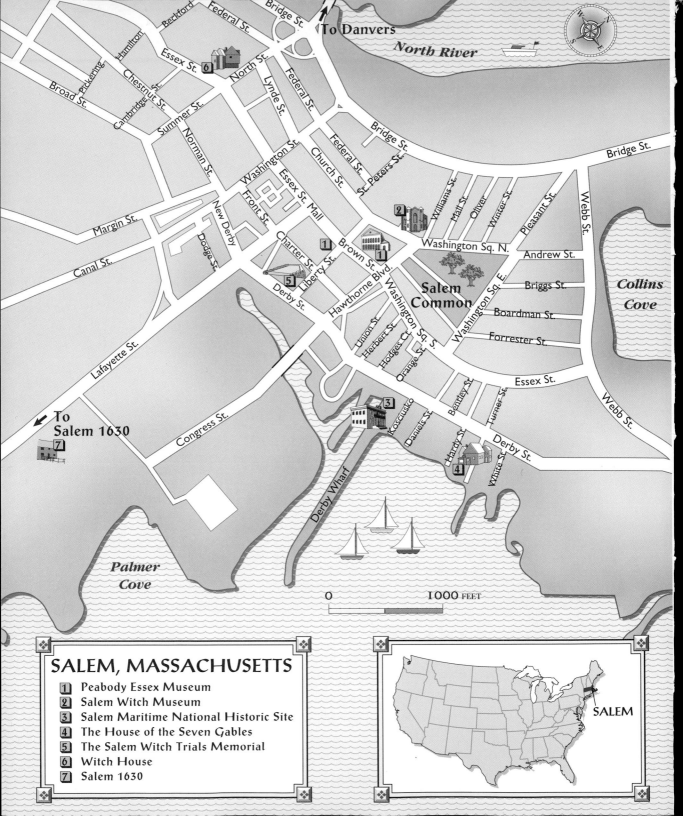

To Danvers

*North River*

**6**

Beckford    Federal St.    Bridge St.

Hamilton    Essex St.

Pickering    Chestnut St.    Summer St.    North St.    Lynde St.    Federal St.    Federal St.    Bridge St.    Bridge St.

Broad St.    Cambridge    Norman St.    Washington St.    Church St.    St. Peters St.

Margin St.    New Derby    Front St.    Essex St. Mall    Williams St.    Mall St.    Oliver St.    Winter St.    Pleasant St.    Webb St.

Canal St.    Dodge St.    Charter St.    Liberty St.    Brown St.    **1**    **2**    Washington Sq. N.

**1**    Andrew St.    *Collins Cove*

**5**    Derby St.    Hawthorne Blvd.    Washington Blvd.    Salem Common    Washington Sq. E.    Briggs St.    Boardman St.

Lafayette St.    Union St.    Herbert St.    Hodges Ct.    Orange St.    Washington Sq. S.    Forrester St.    Essex St.

To Salem 1630    Congress St.    **3**    Kosciusko St.    Daniels St.    Bentley St.    Turner St.    Derby St.    Webb St.

**7**    Derby Wharf    Hardy St.    **4**    White St.

*Palmer Cove*

0    1000 FEET

---

SALEM

# CHAPTER 6

# VISITING SALEM

Today you can walk through the streets of Salem and catch a glimpse into this town's exciting past. Begin your tour at the Salem Witch Museum at 19 1/2 Washington Square North. Here you can see a program that tells the story of the witchcraft hysteria of 1692. The presentation comes alive through a series of illuminated scenes featuring life-size figures.

You can also visit the Witch House at 310 1/2 Essex Street. In 1692 this building was the home of Jonathan Corwin, one of the officials called to Salem Village when the witchcraft hysteria began. Several accused witches were brought to Corwin's home for pretrial questioning. The house is now restored to appear much as it did in 1692.

*The House of the Seven Gables in Salem, built in 1668 by Captain John Turner, later became the famous setting for Nathaniel Hawthorne's novel.*

One of the best-known sites in Salem is The House of the Seven Gables, located at 54 Turner Street. The house was built in the seventeenth century by Captain John Turner, a wealthy shipowner. The author Nathaniel Hawthorne, a descendant of Magistrate John Hathorne, used it as the setting for one of his most famous novels, *The House of the Seven Gables*. Hawthorne's book is based on the story of Reverend Nicholas Noyes, who was cursed by Sarah Good from the

Λ costumed guide at Salem 1630

gallows. One fascinating feature of the house itself is a secret staircase that was discovered during restoration efforts in 1910.

If you'd like to learn more about everyday life in Puritan Massachusetts, then take a tour through Salem 1630 in Forest River Park at the end of West Avenue in Salem. Salem 1630, formerly known as Pioneer Village, is the nation's oldest living-history museum. Tour guides dressed in period costumes recreate the daily life of Salem's people during the 1630s.

*The Peabody Museum in Salem is the nation's oldest museum in continuous operation.*

The Peabody Essex Museum at East India Square is really two museums in one. The Peabody Museum, founded in 1799, is the oldest continuously operating museum in the United States. Its exhibits include historical paintings of ships and maritime scenes as well as examples of the exotic treasures that Salem sea captains brought back from India and China. The Essex

Institute houses many of the original documents
from the witchcraft trials of 1692 and oversees
the management of several historic homes in
Salem.

A visit to the Salem Maritime National
Historic Site at 174 Derby Street includes Derby
Wharf and the port's 1819 custom house, which
is where port officials inspected the documents
and cargoes of overseas trade. Several historic
homes along the shore are also part of this site,
which was established in 1938.

As a fitting end to your visit to Salem, stop
by the Salem Tercentenary Witchcraft Memorial
on Charter Street. This monument, erected in
1992, commemorates the 20 women and men who
lost their lives in the witchcraft panic of 1692.

As another reminder of the many people
whose lives were shattered during the witchcraft
trials, you can visit the homestead of Rebecca
Nurse, located at 149 Pine Street in Danvers,
Massachusetts (formerly Salem Village). Rebecca
Nurse's home has been restored to look much as

it did during her lifetime. On the grounds stands a reconstruction of the old Salem Village Meetinghouse. The body of George Jacobs, who was hanged as a wizard in 1692, lies in the nearby burial ground.

# A Salem Time Line

**1626**   A small band of English Puritan colonists moves to present-day Salem from an unsuccessful settlement at Cape Ann.

**1628**   A larger group of Puritan settlers arrives at Salem from England.

**1630**   Salem becomes part of Massachusetts Bay Colony under Governor John Winthrop.

**1672**   The outlying settlement of Salem Farms becomes the separate parish of Salem Village (present-day Danvers)

**1680**   George Burroughs is hired as the Salem Village preacher.

**1683**   George Burroughs leaves Salem Village.

**1688**   Reverend Samuel Parris arrives to serve as pastor of Salem Village.

**1692**   (January) Betty Parris and Abigail Williams begin to have strange convulsions at the Salem Village parsonage; several other girls develop the same symptoms.

**1692** (February) The afflicted girls accuse three Salem Village women of practicing witchcraft.

**1692** (March through May) More and more girls and young women develop convulsions; dozens of people in Salem and nearby towns are accused of being witches or wizards.

**1692** (June to September) Witchcraft trials are held in Salem; 19 condemned witches are hanged; afflictions and accusations continue throughout the summer.

**1692** (October) Increase Mather calls for an end to the witchcraft panic; Governor Joseph Phips orders that no more unnecessary arrests be made and that accused witches be treated fairly.

**1693** (January) The last witchcraft trials are held; three people are condemned but none hanged.

**1697** Salem ministers call for a day of prayer and fasting to ask forgiveness for the witchcraft executions.

**1706** Anne Putnam asks for forgiveness during service at the Salem Village Meetinghouse.

**1786** Elias Hasket Derby commissions the first Salem vessel to sail to China.

**1790–** The port of Salem enjoys the peak years
**1807** of its trade with China and India.

**1807** The Embargo Act closes Salem and other American ports to foreign trade.

**1809** The embargo is lifted; foreign trade resumes.

**1870** The bark *Glide* is the last sailing ship from Salem to return from a voyage beyond the Cape of Good Hope.

**1937** Salem Customs House closes.

**1938** Salem Customs House, Derby Wharf, and relics of the port of Salem become part of Salem Maritime National Historic Site.

**1992** On the 300th anniversary of the infamous trials, the Salem Tercentenary Witchcraft Memorial is erected to commemorate the women and men who lost their lives in the witchcraft panic of 1692.

# VISITOR INFORMATION

**Salem Witch Museum**—19½ Washington Square
North, Route 1A. Open every day of the year except
Thanksgiving, Christmas, and New Year's Day.
September through June: 10:00 A.M. to 5:00 P.M. July
and August: 10:00 A.M. to 7:00 P.M. For special events
in October tied to Halloween, the museum is sometimes open until midnight. Admission: children, $2.50;
adults, $4; senior citizens, $3.50. (508) 744-1692.

**Witch House**—310½ Essex Street. Open March 15
through December 1: 10:00 A.M. to 4:30 P.M. July 1
through Labor Day: 10:00 A.M. to 6:00 P.M. Admission:
$4 for individuals; $3 for members of a group of 15 or
more. Guided tours are available. (508) 744-0180.

**The House of the Seven Gables**—54 Turner Street.
Open seven days a week. November 1 through June
30: 10:00 A.M. to 4:30 P.M.; July 1 through October 31:
9:00 A.M. to 6:00 P.M. Admission: children under 6,
free; children 6–12, $3; children 13–17, $4; adults,
$7. (508) 744-0991.

**Salem 1630**—Forest River Park (mailing address, 54
Turner Street). Open Memorial Day weekend
through October 31. 10:00 A.M. to 5:00 P.M. Monday
through Saturday; noon to 5:00 P.M. Sunday.
Admission: children under 6, free; children 6–12,

$2.50; children 13–17, $3.50; adults, $4.50; special family and group rates available. (508) 744-0991.

**Peabody Essex Museum**—East India Square. April through November: Monday through Saturday, 10:00 A.M. to 5:00 P.M.; Sunday, noon to 5:00 P.M. December through March: same hours, but closed Mondays. Admission: children under 5, free; children 5–16, $4; adults, $7; seniors and students, $6; family and group rates available. Guided tours of the museum and of three historic houses can be arranged. (508) 745-1876.

**Salem Maritime National Historic Site**—174 Derby Street. Open seven days a week. January through April: 10:00 A.M. to 5:00 P.M. May through December: 8:30 A.M. to 5:00 P.M. Admission is free.

**Salem Tercentenary Witchcraft Memorial**—Liberty Street between Derby and Charter. An outdoor monument, open year-round. Admission is free.

**Rebecca Nurse Homestead**—149 Pine Street, Danvers. Open June 15 to October 31. June 15 to Labor Day: Tuesday through Sunday, 1:00 P.M. to 4:30 P.M. September and October: Saturday and Sunday, 1:00 P.M. to 4:30 P.M. Admission: Children, $2; adults, $3.50.

# INDEX